Rik's Hill

Written by Tanya Luther

Illustrated by Kristen Humphrey

Rik's hill is a mess.

I will visit Red and Dot's pond!

Rik gets his fig.

Figs can be big!

Rik huffs
and puffs.

I must drop
the fig and
go on.

Rik sits.
Dot naps.

At last,
Red is back.

Red drops
the fig!

Dot's pad is wet.

q

Red gets the fig.

Red pecks. Rik licks.

Can I get a bit?